Thinking Critically: Fossil Fuels

Other titles in the *Thinking Critically* series include:

Thinking Critically: Fossil Fuels

Bradley Steffens

ReferencePoint Press®

San Diego, CA

© 2019 ReferencePoint Press, Inc.
Printed in the United States

For more information, contact:
ReferencePoint Press, Inc.
PO Box 27779
San Diego, CA 92198
www.ReferencePointPress.com

Picture Credits:
Cover: Red Squirrel/Shutterstock.com
10: iStockphoto.com
Illustrations by Maury Aaseng

LIBRARY OF CONGRESS CATALOGING-IN-PUBLICATION DATA

Name: Steffens, Bradley, 1955– author.
Title: Thinking Critically: Fossil Fuels/by Bradley Steffens.
Other titles: Fossil Fuels
Description: San Diego, CA: ReferencePoint Press, Inc., 2019. | Series: Thinking Critically |
    Audience: Grade 9 to 12. | Includes bibliographical references and index.
Identifiers: LCCN 2018040175 (print) | LCCN 2018046061 (ebook) | ISBN 9781682825341 (eBook)
    | ISBN 9781682825334 (hardback)
Subjects: LCSH: Fossil fuels—Juvenile literature.
Classification: LCC TP318.3 (ebook) | LCC TP318.3 .S74 2019 (print) | DDC 662.6—dc23
LC record available at https://lccn.loc.gov/2018040175

Contents

Foreword

"Literacy is the most basic currency of the knowledge economy we're living in today." Barack Obama (at the time a senator from Illinois) spoke these words during a 2005 speech before the American Library Association. One question raised by this statement is: What does it mean to be a literate person in the twenty-first century?

E.D. Hirsch Jr., author of *Cultural Literacy: What Every American Needs to Know*, answers the question this way: "To be culturally literate is to possess the basic information needed to thrive in the modern world. The breadth of the information is great, extending over the major domains of human activity from sports to science."

But literacy in the twenty-first century goes beyond the accumulation of knowledge gained through study and experience and expanded over time. Now more than ever literacy requires the ability to sift through and evaluate vast amounts of information and, as the authors of the Common Core State Standards state, to "demonstrate the cogent reasoning and use of evidence that is essential to both private deliberation and responsible citizenship in a democratic republic."

The *Thinking Critically* series challenges students to become discerning readers, to think independently, and to engage and develop their skills as critical thinkers. Through a narrative-driven, pro/con format, the series introduces students to the complex issues that dominate public discourse—topics such as gun control and violence, social networking, and medical marijuana. Each chapter revolves around a single, pointed question such as Can Stronger Gun Control Measures Prevent Mass Shootings?, or Does Social Networking Benefit Society?, or Should Medical Marijuana Be Legalized? This inquiry-based approach introduces student researchers to core issues and concerns on a given topic. Each chapter includes one part that argues the affirmative and one part that argues the negative—all written by a single author. With the single-author format the predominant arguments for and against an issue can be synthesized into clear, accessible discussions supported by details and evidence including relevant facts, direct quotes, current examples, and statistical illustrations. All volumes include focus questions to guide students as they read each pro/con discussion, a list of key facts, and an annotated list of related organizations and websites for conducting further research.

The authors of the Common Core State Standards have set out the particular qualities that a literate person in the twenty-first century must have. These include the ability to think independently, establish a base of knowledge across a wide range of subjects, engage in open-minded but discerning reading and listening, know how to use and evaluate evidence, and appreciate and understand diverse perspectives. The new *Thinking Critically* series supports these goals by providing a solid introduction to the study of pro/con issues.

Fossil Fuels

Since the 1780s, when coal surpassed wood as the world's chief source of energy, fossil fuels—coal, petroleum, and natural gas—have powered the industrial world. In 2017 fossil fuels accounted for 85 percent of total global energy consumption. Only 10 percent of the world's energy came from renewable sources, such as solar, wind, biomass, biofuels, and hydroelectric. The remaining 5 percent came from nuclear power. In the United States fossil fuels account for 80 percent of the energy consumption, renewables account for 11 percent, and nuclear power accounts for 9 percent. This is according to the US Energy Information Administration (EIA), an agency of the federal government responsible for ongoing energy analysis and communication. Fossil fuels power much of the electrical grid and the lights and machines connected to it. They also power all of the world's commercial and military aircraft and the vast majority of its automobiles, ships, and trains.

A Surge in Fossil Fuel Production

For decades experts have been predicting that the world would soon run out of fossil fuels, but this has not happened. In 1957 geologist M. King Hubbert predicted that US oil production would peak at about 3 billion barrels per year around 1970 and then decline to about 450 million barrels per year by 2017. Hubbert's oil production model became known as Hubbert's curve, and his theory became known as peak oil production, or peak oil. Although US oil production did reach a peak of 3.5 billion barrels in 1970, it has not declined according to Hubbert's prediction. In fact, US oil production reached 3.4 billion barrels per year in 2017—7.5 times more than Hubbert's curve predicted for this time. The EIA projected that US production would reach an all-time high of 3.7 billion barrels per year in 2018 and then surpass 4 billion barrels per year in 2019. This surge in oil production has made the United States the world's largest crude oil producer, surpassing Russia and Saudi Arabia in 2018, according to the EIA.

The Advent of Fracking

The primary reason for the increase in US fossil fuel production has been the ability of fossil fuel producers to remove oil and natural gas liquids from shale and other rock formations at a competitive price. This is possible because of horizontal drilling and a process known as hydraulic fracturing, or fracking. This process breaks the rock into pieces and uses extreme pressure to force the fossil fuels out of the rock. The EIA reports that half of US crude oil produced in 2017 came from fracking.

Fracking also allows energy companies to capture large amounts of natural gas. The EIA reports that US natural gas production reached a record high of 90.9 billion cubic feet (2.57 billion cu. m) per day in 2017, more than half of which came from fracking. The United States now leads all countries in the production of natural gas. Fracking helped push the global production of natural gas to a new record of 355 billion cubic feet (10 billion cu. m) per day in 2017, an increase of 3 percent over 2016.

While oil and natural gas production are soaring, the use of fossil fuels is not. Global fossil fuel use increased by less than 1 percent in 2017. This is mainly because the demand for coal has dropped in the United States and Europe. The US consumption of coal has declined by an astounding 38 percent since 2005. As a result, the 80 percent fossil fuel share of US energy consumption in 2017 was the lowest fossil fuel share since 1902. Meanwhile, the share of energy generated by renewable sources, including wind turbines, solar panels, and hydroelectric dams, has risen to its highest level since the 1910s, when the main renewable was wood.

Fossil Fuels and Climate Change

The most important reason for the decline in the use of fossil fuels is concern about the effects they have on the environment. When fossil

Fossil fuels are the primary source of power for electricity production and global transportation. They are also a major producer of carbon dioxide, an atmospheric gas that scientists say is trapping the sun's heat, warming the planet, and driving a change in the world's climate.

fuels burn, they produce large amounts of carbon dioxide (CO_2), an atmospheric gas that scientists say is trapping the sun's heat, warming parts of the planet, and driving a change in the world's climate. The polar ice caps and glaciers are melting, and that is raising sea levels around the world. The global sea level has risen by about 8 inches (20.3 cm) since 1880. Ice on frozen rivers and lakes is breaking up earlier in the year than it used to, and trees are flowering sooner. According to the Intergovernmental Panel on Climate Change (IPCC), the United Nations task force dedicated to providing a scientific view of climate change, CO_2 emissions from the burning of fossil fuels and industrial processes contributed about 78 percent of the total greenhouse gas emissions increase from 1970 to 2010. "Their effects, together with those of other anthropogenic [human-caused] drivers, have been detected throughout the climate system and are extremely likely to have been the dominant cause of the observed warming since the mid-20th century,"[1] states the IPCC.

A small number of scientists are not so sure that fossil fuels are actually causing climate change. "The changes observed over the last several decades are likely mostly due to human activities, but we cannot rule out that some significant part of these changes is also a reflection of natural variability,"[2] states the National Academy of Sciences, a nonprofit organization charged by Congress to provide advice to the nation on matters related to science and technology. Various natural phenomena may be behind the observed changes in the climate. For example, ocean currents affect global temperatures. A 2017 National Aeronautics and Space Administration (NASA) study using satellite data found that the climate cycle known as El Niño drove average global temperatures to three straight annual records. Not all sea level changes are related to human activity, either. In June 2018 scientists from the University of Rhode Island discovered an active volcano beneath Antarctica's Pine Island Glacier, the fastest-melting glacier in Antarctica and the single-biggest contributor to global sea level rise. Scientists had attributed the glacier's rapid loss of ice to global warming, but the new study reveals that the active volcano beneath the glacier is causing much of the melting.

> "[Fossil fuel] effects, together with those of other anthropogenic [human-caused] drivers, have been detected throughout the climate system and are extremely likely to have been the dominant cause of the observed warming since the mid-20th century."[1]
>
> —The IPCC, a United Nations task force that provides a scientific view of climate change

Reducing CO_2 Emissions

Concern about CO_2 emissions is one reason that natural gas has surpassed coal as the leading source of electrical power generation in the United States. Natural gas emits about half as much CO_2 when it burns as coal does. By switching from coal to natural gas to generate electricity, the United States has led the world in the reduction of CO_2 emissions for ten straight years. Energy-related CO_2 emissions declined by 14 percent—949 million tons (861 million metric tons)—from 2005 to 2017, according to the EIA. However, CO_2 emissions grew globally, in part because China's CO_2 emissions increased by 3.3 billion tons (3 billion metric tons) and India's grew by 1.1 billion tons (1 billion metric tons) during the same period.

Some experts are not that impressed with the reduction in US CO_2 emissions. They point out that even with its CO_2 reductions, the United States still produces more CO_2 emissions than any other country in the world except China, emitting 5.6 billion tons (5 billion metric tons) of CO_2 per year, according to the World Bank. China emits almost twice as much, 10.2 billion tons (9.25 billion metric tons) per year, but it has four times as many people. On a per-person basis, the United States produces more than double the emissions of China and eight times more than India. "The United States has a long way to go to bring per capita emissions in line with China and India,"[3] comments Nicole Lewis, a reporter for the *Washington Post*'s Fact Checker column.

A Major Source of Pollution

Fossil fuels have also fallen out of favor because they are a major source of air, water, and soil pollution. Oil spills like the *Deepwater Horizon* disaster of 2010, which spewed 4 million barrels of oil into the Gulf of Mexico, have fouled thousands of miles of coastline and killed millions of birds and sea animals.

When fossil fuels are burned, they release toxic gases and chemicals into the air. These include carbon monoxide and nitrogen oxides. In the presence of sunlight, nitrogen oxides can combine with other chemicals in the atmosphere to create ozone, a harmful pollutant that causes respiratory illnesses. The World Health Organization says that 4 million people die each year from breathing outdoor air pollution, mainly caused by the burning of fossil fuels.

Since the 1980s the industrialized nations of Europe and North America have made an effort to move away from the use of fossil fuels in order to reduce pollution and slow or even stop climate change. At the same time, fossil fuels remain vital to their economies and standards of living. Controversy continues to surround the use of fossil fuels today and the role they will play in the future.

Chapter One

Should the World Stop Using Fossil Fuels?

The World Should Not Stop Using Fossil Fuels

- The world's growing demand for energy can only be met by fossil fuels.
- Fossil fuels are cheaper than alternative sources of energy.
- Unlike renewable energy sources, fossil fuels are a reliable power source in any climate and in any weather.

The Debate at a Glance

The World Should Stop Using Fossil Fuels

- Fossils fuels are the chief source of greenhouse gases and pollution.
- Energy from most fossil fuels now costs more than energy from renewable sources.
- The cost of fossil fuels will rise in the future, while the cost of renewables will fall.
- The amount of fossil fuels is finite, and the world will soon run out of them.

The World Should Not Stop Using Fossil Fuels

"Fossil fuels are the life blood of the economy and essential for economic development."

—William O'Keefe, chief executive officer of the George C. Marshall Institute, a nonprofit think tank

William O'Keefe, interview with the author, September 10, 2018.

Consider these questions as you read:

1. Do you think countries that used fossil fuels to develop their economies have the right to tell still-developing countries that they cannot use fossil fuels to do the same? Why or why not?
2. Do you believe fossil fuels should be part of the world's energy mix? Why or why not?
3. When comparing fossil fuels with renewable power sources, how much importance should be given to cost and reliability? Explain your answer.

Editor's note: The discussion that follows presents common arguments made in support of this perspective, reinforced by facts, quotes, and examples taken from various sources.

The vast majority of climate scientists believe that fossil fuels are the major cause of increased levels of CO_2 in the atmosphere and the climate change that is taking place around the globe. Accordingly, many people are calling for an end to the use of fossil fuels. This is understandable but misguided. The cost of moving away from fossil fuels—not just in dollars, but also in the quality of life and even in lives themselves—is too high even to consider.

Energy for Economic Progress

The world's population is growing, and the world's demand for energy is growing with it. According to the EIA, total world energy consumption will increase by 28 percent by 2040. More than half of that growth will occur in Asia as poor countries try to raise their standards of living. Where will this new energy come from? The short answer is fossil fuels.

Currently, there are sixteen hundred new coal plants planned or under construction in sixty-two countries, according to the Global Coal Plant Tracker portal. The new plants will expand the world's coal-fired power capacity by 43 percent. Some people believe the increased use of fossil fuels in Asia poses a danger to the environment, but it is wrong to argue that the people of these countries should not have access to the same labor-saving, health-preserving technologies that people in the West take for granted. Lights, appliances, heating and air-conditioning, hospital equipment, transportation, and even running water all require energy to operate. "People who want to curb the use of fossil fuels need to understand that not everyone in the world has the luxury of inventing romanticized scenarios," says Lee R. Raymond, the president of Mobil Holdings in the United Kingdom. "Many people just need clean water and energy to fuel social and economic progress."[4]

A Unique Resource

Great strides have been made in the production of electricity from renewable sources such as solar and wind power, but these sources of power fall far short of meeting the world's energy needs. According to the Renewable Energy Policy Network for the 21st Century, a global renewable energy think tank, wind and solar technologies produce 5.5 percent of the world's electricity today. But the world needs more than electricity. When transportation, home heating, and industry are factored in, the share of wind and solar is a minuscule 1.6 percent of the world's total energy supply. Other renewables, such as hydroelectric dams, make up 17.7 percent of the world's energy supply, for a total of 19.3 percent. About half of that, however, is traditional biomass, a fancy term for burning wood, which is renewable but not clean. Nuclear power makes up

Fossil Fuels Continue to Be an Essential Energy Source

Fossil fuels, particularly oil and natural gas, are and will be an essential energy source at least until 2050—and probably well beyond that date. According to projections by the US Energy Information Administration, fossil fuels will continue to dominate US energy consumption for the foreseeable future. Although coal's dominance has slipped, oil, natural gas, and coal combined will still provide about 77 percent of US energy in 2050. Clearly, fossil fuels remain an important part of the energy mix.

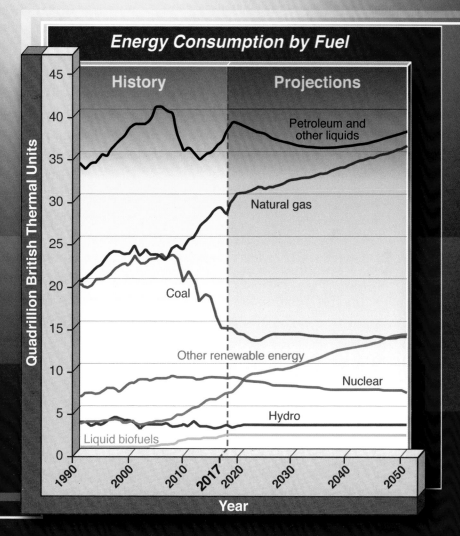

Energy Consumption by Fuel

History

Projections

Petroleum and other liquids

Natural gas

Coal

Other renewable energy

Nuclear

Hydro

Liquid biofuels

Quadrillion British Thermal Units

Year

Note: British thermal units, or BTUs, are the standard measurement for energy another 2.3 percent of the world's power. That leaves fossil fuels meeting about 80 percent of the world's energy needs today.

The picture will not change drastically in the future. China is currently building twenty-eight new nuclear power plants, and more are being built in India, Russia, and South Korea. However, about one hundred older nuclear power plants will be closed in Europe and the United States over the next two decades, keeping the nuclear share of global energy at about the same level that it is now. Although the consumption of non-fossil fuels is expected to grow faster than fossil fuels in the next decades, the EIA predicts that fossil fuels will still account for 77 percent of the world's energy use in 2040, down just 3 percent from current levels. "It seems impossible to eliminate fossil fuels from the energy mix in the foreseeable future,"[5] states the *Economist*.

> "It seems impossible to eliminate fossil fuels from the energy mix in the foreseeable future."[5]
>
> —*The Economist*

Weak Alternatives

Renewable resources may be fine for generating electricity for homes and office buildings, but it cannot be used to power heavy machinery or the bulk of the world's transportation needs. Today's massive ships cannot be powered solely by batteries or solar panels. Neither can freight trains or jumbo jets. These machines need concentrated sources of power that can perform anywhere, from thousands of miles at sea to thousands of feet in the air. Right now, only petroleum products—gasoline, diesel fuel, and jet fuel—can provide that kind of mobility and power. That is why petroleum currently accounts for the largest share of all energy consumption, 37 percent, and will remain the largest share past 2050, according to the EIA.

The United States is now producing about twice as much oil and gas as it was ten years ago. "Over the past decade, merely the increase—I repeat, just the increase—in US oil and gas production is equal to seven times the total energy production of every wind turbine and solar project

18

in the United States," writes Robert Bryce, a senior fellow at the Manhattan Institute, a conservative think tank. From 2008 to 2018, US oil and gas output increased by about 10.5 million barrels of oil equivalent per day, while wind and solar increased by 1.5 million barrels of oil equivalent per day. "Simple division (10.5 divided by 1.5) shows that since 2008, the increase in energy production from oil and gas is equal to seven times the energy output of all domestic solar and wind,"[6] says Bryce.

Fossil fuels also are a cheaper source of electric power than renewables. In 2017 the cost of generating power from an existing coal plant was just 4 cents per kilowatt-hour (kWh), compared to 6 to 7 cents per kWh for wind power. (A kilowatt-hour is the amount of energy consumed in an hour by a device continuously using 1 kilowatt of power.) Even when computing the cost of energy from a new power plant, rather than from an existing plant, natural gas is still cheaper than solar and wind. According to the EIA, the median cost of energy from a new solar thermal plant is 24 cents per kWh, three times higher than the average cost of energy from a new natural gas plant, which is just 7.3 cents per kWh. The cost of energy from a new photovoltaic solar farm is 12.5 cents per kWh. That is 42 percent more costly than energy from a new natural gas plant. Energy sources that cost consumers more will lose out in the marketplace.

> "Alternative energy systems alone will not be capable of meeting the baseload generation needs of a developed economy for the foreseeable future."[8]
>
> —Lazard, a global financial advisory and asset management firm

Because of its low cost, natural gas already makes up more of the US energy mix (29 percent) than all renewables combined (19 percent). Natural gas is vital to the world's expanding economies. The EIA says that natural gas will be the fastest-growing fossil fuel of the next twenty years worldwide, with global consumption increasing by 30 percent between 2015 and 2040. With growth like that, it will take several decades at least for renewables to catch up to fossil fuels. In the meantime, the world needs more energy. As recently as 2016, 1.5 billion of the world's 7.3 billion people had no electricity. Many of these people rely on wood burning for heat and light. As Matt Ridley, a member of the British Parliament, points out, "This is not just an inconvenience for them: Indoor air pollution from wood fires kills four million people a year."[7] That must change.

A Reliable Resource

Besides being cheap, fossil fuels are reliable. They can generate power in any region, in any climate, and in any weather. By contrast, hydroelectric plants have to be built on rivers, solar farms need to be built in sunny areas, and wind farms must be located where strong winds blow. Even geothermal is susceptible to the whims of nature. In May 2018 lava flows from the Kilauea volcano on the island of Hawaii led to the shutdown of the Puna Geothermal Venture power plant, which produces about 29 percent of the island's electricity. "Alternative energy systems alone will not be capable of meeting the baseload generation needs of a developed economy for the foreseeable future," states Lazard, a global financial advisory firm. "Therefore, the optimal solution for many regions of the world is to use complementary conventional and alternative energy resources."[8] Conventional energy resources, of course, means fossil fuels.

The World Should Stop Using Fossil Fuels

"Human activity is overloading our atmosphere with carbon dioxide and other global warming emissions. These gases act like a blanket, trapping heat. The result is a web of significant and harmful impacts, from stronger, more frequent storms, to drought, sea level rise, and extinction."

—Union of Concerned Scientists

"Benefits of Renewable Energy Use," Union of Concerned Scientists, December 20, 2017. www.ucsusa.org.

Consider these questions as you read:

1. Do you believe the role of fossil fuels in climate change is reason enough for the world to stop using them? Why or why not?
2. Why does cost matter in the debate over ending global dependence on fossil fuels?
3. Do you believe a world without fossil fuels is possible? Why or why not?

Editor's note: The discussion that follows presents common arguments made in support of this perspective, reinforced by facts, quotes, and examples taken from various sources.

The burning of fossil fuels is the greatest single contributor to the rise in global CO_2 emissions, which scientists agree is causing climate change. To avert the violent weather and rising sea levels that climate change will bring, scientists are urging global adoption of cleaner sources of energy. "Humanity's effect on the Earth system, through the large-scale combustion of fossil fuels and widespread deforestation and the resulting release of carbon dioxide (CO_2) into the atmosphere . . . is unprecedented,"

Renewable Energy Should Be Higher Priority than Fossil Fuels

A majority of Americans favor development of renewable energy sources over expanded production of fossil fuels—a sentiment that has been steadily growing over time. This is the finding of a series of polls by the Pew Research Center. The latest of these polls, conducted in 2017, reveals that two-thirds of US adults now believe that developing renewable energy should be a national priority—the highest number on record. Only 27 percent think that developing fossil fuels should be a priority.

Percent of US adults who say _____ should be the more important priority for addressing America's energy supply

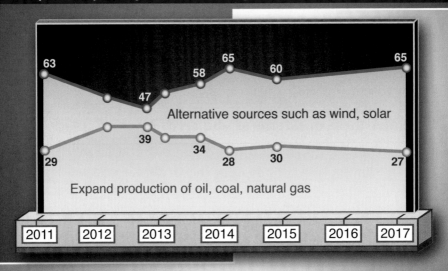

Source: Pew Research Center, "Two-Thirds of Americans Give Priority to Developing Alternative Energy Over Fossil Fuels," Brian Kennedy, January 23, 2017. www.pewresearch.org.

states the US Global Change Research Program. Human activities, the organization continues, "are driving changes in temperature and other climate variables."[9] People worldwide must stop using fossil fuels sooner rather than later to avert the coming climate disaster.

Losing the Cost Battle

Defenders of fossil fuels argue that the world cannot afford to move away from so-called dirty energy because of the high cost of clean technologies such as solar and wind power. This was true in the past, but renewables have recently become cheaper than fossil fuels. For example, a 2017 report from Lazard finds that the cost of energy from a new wind power plant fell 67 percent from 2009 to 2017, from 13.5 cents per kWh to just 4.5 cents per kWh. Meanwhile, the median cost of energy from solar farms fell an astounding 86 percent during the same period, from 35.8 cents per kWh to just 4.9 cents per kWh. "In some scenarios the full-lifecycle costs of building and operating renewables-based projects have dropped below the operating costs alone of conventional generation technologies such as coal or nuclear,"[10] states Lazard.

Energy from fossil fuels is now more expensive than energy from solar and wind, according to Lazard. The firm places the median cost of energy from a new coal-fired electric plant at 10.1 cents per kWh—more than double the cost of solar energy. The median cost of energy from a new natural gas power plant is 6 cents per kilowatt, or about 25 percent more than the cost of wind power and 18 percent more than the cost of solar.

The greatest demand for new energy is coming from the developing world. In these regions, renewables are an even better bargain because companies can build large wind and solar farms with lower labor costs. The developing world is putting its money into renewable sources to meet its urgent energy needs. In 2015 the developing nations surpassed the developed nations in spending on new renewable energy sources for the first time, spending $154.1 billion on renewables compared with $153.7 billion by the wealthier countries. "Renewable energy will beat any other technology in most of the world without subsidies," says Michael Liebreich, chair of Bloomberg New Energy Finance. For example, a 2016 auction among companies competing to provide energy to Chile led to a deal to provide solar energy for a record low 2.9 cents per kWh. "Renewables are robustly entering the era of undercutting"[11] fossil fuel prices, says Liebreich.

> "Renewable energy will beat any other technology in most of the world without subsidies."[11]
>
> —Michael Liebreich, chair of Bloomberg New Energy Finance

A Dwindling Resource

The trend toward renewables will continue because fossil fuels will only become more expensive in the future. This is because there is a limited supply of fossil fuels. They were created through millions of years of geological pressures. Once they are used, they are gone forever. As the supply dwindles, the cost of the remaining fossil fuels will rise dramatically.

Fossil fuel costs will rise soon because even though supplies exist, they are more difficult to recover and therefore more costly. The nearby, easily accessible reserves of oil and gas are being depleted. As a result, energy companies must venture into new areas to extract untapped supplies. This means drilling in ever deeper waters and setting up operations in increasingly inhospitable regions such as the Arctic to obtain new supplies. The cost of recovering such reserves will be much higher than the cost of existing resources, and those costs will be passed on to the consumer. The higher fossil fuel costs will make renewable energy a bargain.

While the cost of developing new fossil fuel resources is rising, the cost of developing new renewable energy sources is falling fast. The cost of photovoltaic solar panels has decreased two hundredfold since they were introduced in the late 1970s, from seventy-seven dollars per watt in 1977 to just thirty-seven cents per watt in 2018, according to Bloomberg New Energy Finance. The firm predicts the cost will fall even further, to twenty-one cents per watt in 2040. "With renewables, costs have really fallen much faster than even we anticipated a few years ago," says Jenny Chase, head of solar analysis at Bloomberg New Energy Finance. "I've been a solar analyst since 2006, and if I had published a totally accurate forecast of how much solar costs have decreased since then, everyone would have thought I was completely crazy."[12]

Because of the falling prices of renewables and their role in reducing carbon emissions, solar and wind technologies will account for 64 percent of the total electric generation growth between 2017 and 2040, according to the EIA. The agency predicts that electrical generation from renewables will more than double between 2017 and 2050, from about 700 billion kWh to 1,400 billion kWh. Renewables will surpass both nuclear power and coal as a source of electrical power in the United States by 2040.

The Future Belongs to Renewables

Fossil fuels will also lose their share of the transportation market. According to the EIA, the share of sales of gasoline and flex-fuel vehicles (which use a blend of gasoline and ethanol) in the United States will decline from 95 percent in 2017 to 78 percent in 2050. The loss of market share will be due mainly to the increasing popularity of electric cars. The sales of electric and hybrid vehicles (which normally use electric battery power to accelerate and then switch over to gasoline, diesel, or flex fuels to cruise) will grow in market share from 4 percent in 2017 to 19 percent in 2050, says the EIA. In addition, hybrid buses, trains, and even ships are cutting into the fossil fuel market. Beginning in 2019 the Color Hybrid ferry will carry up to 2,000 passengers and approximately 450 vehicles between Norway and Sweden. "Battery-powered propulsion in ships this size shows that batteries are onboard to stay," says Frederic Hauge, founder and president of environmental group Bellona. "This represents a huge reduction in emissions from shipping, and it is only the beginning."[13]

> "My guess is probably in 10 years more than half of new vehicle production is electric in the United States."[14]
>
> —Elon Musk, CEO of Tesla

Elon Musk, the founder and chief executive officer (CEO) of electric automaker Tesla, believes the EIA's forecast of the growth of the electric car market is far too conservative. In July 2017 he told the National Governors Association, "I think things are going to grow exponentially. . . . My guess is probably in 10 years more than half of new vehicle production is electric in the United States."[14]

Musk is not alone in his belief that the growth in electric automobile sales will exceed the EIA estimates. In 2017 analysts at financial services giant Morgan Stanley also predicted electric cars would surpass gasoline-powered cars in market share, but they said it would not occur until 2040. The firm predicted that electric cars would account for 16 percent of the automobile market by 2030, 51 percent by 2040, and 69 percent by 2050. The firm suggests that with added government pressure to reduce auto emissions, the share of electric cars could reach 90 percent by 2045.

If the estimates about electric cars are right, fossil fuel consumption will fall at an even faster rate. Today more than 34 percent of US energy consumption comes from liquid petroleum, and 54 percent of that is used for transportation. If the gasoline-powered internal combustion engine becomes all but obsolete by 2050, total fossil fuel consumption could plunge by another 10 percent to 15 percent. That would be a good thing for consumers and an even better thing for the planet.

Chapter Two

Is Fracking a Good Way to Produce Fossil Fuels?

Fracking Is a Good Way to Produce Fossil Fuels

- By reducing the need for imported oil and gas, fracking has made US energy independent and enhanced security at home and abroad.
- Fracking boosts the economy by driving down the cost of natural gas and oil and by creating new jobs.
- Fracking increases the supply of natural gas, the cleanest fossil fuel.

The Debate at a Glance

Fracking Is Not a Good Way to Produce Fossil Fuels

- Fracking pollutes the water and air.
- Fracking endangers human health.
- Fracking triggers potentially dangerous earthquakes.

Fracking Is a Good Way to Produce Fossil Fuels

"America is reducing emissions because of affordable abundant natural gas made possible by fracking, which has also helped U.S. GDP [gross domestic product] grow 20.4 percent since 2005. No other major industrialized country can boast this historic and unprecedented decoupling trend."

—Seth Whitehead, team lead for Energy In Depth, an outreach and education program sponsored by the Independent Petroleum Association of America

Seth Whitehead, "EIA: U.S. Carbon Emissions Fall Again in 2017, 'Mainly' Because of Natural Gas," Energy In Depth, February 12, 2018. http://eidclimate.org.

Consider these questions as you read:

1. How important is it that the United States has achieved energy independence through fracking? Explain your answer.
2. Do you believe the economic benefits of fracking outweigh the environmental concerns associated with fossil fuels in general and fracking in particular? Explain your answer.
3. Do you view fracking's role in increasing natural gas and reducing coal and oil as a benefit to society? Why or why not?

Editor's note: The discussion that follows presents common arguments made in support of this perspective, reinforced by facts, quotes, and examples taken from various sources.

In October 2016 drillers with Chesapeake Energy Corporation pumped 25,000 tons (22,680 metric tons) of sand under extreme pressure down a 9,673-foot (2,948 m) natural gas well in Haynesville, Louisiana. The massive infusion of sand fractured the surrounding rock, releasing enormous amounts of natural gas that had been trapped inside the shale rock for millions of years. Well output rose 70 percent after the operation. It was not the first time this technique, known as hydraulic fracturing, or fracking, has been used to extract fossil fuels, but it did set a record for the amount of sand used per foot of a well. Most drillers use 1,500 to 2,000 pounds (680 to 907 kg) per foot. The Chesapeake drillers used 5,100 pounds (2,313 kg) per foot. "What we're doing is unleashing hell on every gas molecule downhole,"[15] said Jason Pigott, Chesapeake's vice president of operations.

Achieving Energy Independence

Fracking is one of those once-in-a-lifetime technologies that changes not only an industry but also history. Before drillers began using fracking to release oil and gas from shale deposits, the United States was importing 70 percent of the oil it consumed. That means it was obtaining most of its oil from other countries. Most of this oil came from the Middle East, an area wracked by conflict and political upheavals, leaving the United States vulnerable to crippling disruptions in supply. Because of fracking, US oil production has doubled since 2008, from 5.2 million barrels per day to 10.2 million barrels per day in 2018. Natural gas production has soared from 55.1 billion cubic feet (1.56 billion cu. m) per day in 2008 to 87.6 billion cubic feet (2.48 billion cu. m) per day in 2018, an increase of about 60 percent. "The

> "The magnitude and velocity of the shale revolution is still underappreciated. Quite simply, it was the fastest and biggest addition to world energy supply that has ever occurred in history."[16]
>
> —Mark P. Mills, an energy analyst with the Manhattan Institute

magnitude and velocity of the shale revolution is still underappreciated," says Mark P. Mills of the Manhattan Institute, an economic think tank. "Quite simply, it was the fastest and biggest addition to world energy supply that has ever occurred in history."[16] Thanks to fracking, the United States is now importing just 19 percent of its oil, mostly from Canada.

Oil is not just a source of industrial power; it is also a source of

A Robust Natural Gas Supply Depends on Fracking

America's natural gas supplies are rapidly growing and becoming cheaper thanks to the advent of fracking. Both shale gas (gas trapped inside shale rock) and tight gas (gas trapped inside other kinds of rock, including sandstone and limestone) are extracted using fracking. Fracking and horizontal drilling will account for 70 percent of US natural gas production in 2040, according to US Energy Information Administration estimates. This represents a 50 percent increase since 2015.

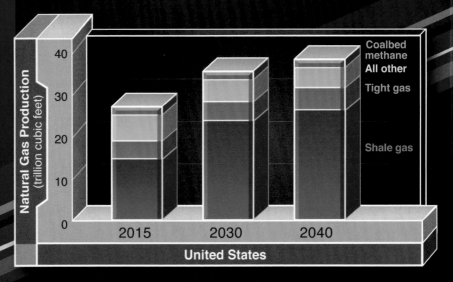

Source: US Energy Information Administration, "Annual Energy Outlook 2017," September 14, 2017, p. 55. www.eia.gov.

political power. By producing most if not all of the oil and natural gas it needs, the United States has become energy independent. This means it no longer has to rely on oil from foreign powers that might turn against it. For example, Middle Eastern oil-producing nations were angered by America's support of Israel in the 1973 Yom Kippur War. To punish the United States for its stance, the Organization of the Petroleum Exporting Countries (OPEC) cut off US oil shipments. Within six months, oil prices quadrupled from $2.90 per barrel to $11.65 per barrel. American service stations began to run out of gasoline, and frightened motorists lined up for blocks to fill their tanks where gas was available. Some states introduced gas rationing using license plate numbers. People whose plates ended with odd numbers could buy gas only on odd-numbered days. People whose plates ended with even numbers could only buy gas on even-numbered days. Consumer spending and industrial production fell, and the US economy slid into a recession. OPEC lifted its embargo in 1974, but the United States remained vulnerable to the political whims of foreign oil suppliers for decades.

Fracking has changed all of that. In February 2018 the United States eclipsed Saudi Arabia as the world's second-largest oil producer, and in August 2018 it surpassed Russia as the world's number one oil producer. By achieving energy independence, the United States is a more secure nation. Its leaders can make decisions based on what is best for the country without fear of reprisals from foreign suppliers of oil.

America's energy independence also means that the country can be a better friend to its allies. Based on projections by the EIA, by 2019 the United States was expected to be exporting more fossil fuel products than it imports for the first time since 1953. As an exporter, the United States can offer reassurances to allies dependent on other foreign sources of oil and gas that it will help them if their current supplies are cut off or reduced. The United States can also offer fossil fuels as incentives for countries to have friendlier relations. Energy independence "puts us in a stronger position to have conversations with countries around the world,"[17] says Jason Bordoff, director of Columbia University's Center on Global Energy Policy. Fracking has helped restore American power abroad.

Fueling an Economic Boom

Fracking is also having a positive impact at home. Not all petroleum is burned for energy. It is also used in the production of plastics and many other products, including health products and cosmetics. Because of the surge in oil production, since 2014 foreign and domestic companies have invested about $160 billion in new chemical-manufacturing facilities in the United States.

Cheap energy lowers the cost of doing business outside the energy sector as well, making businesses with high utility costs more profitable and fueling their growth. This creates more jobs and drives up wages. A 2016 study by IHS Markit, a global financial information provider based in London, found that lower natural gas prices have created about 1.4 million jobs and increased disposable income by about $156 billion in the United States.

The expanding fracking industry has brought tens of thousands of high-paying oil production jobs to rural communities. The increase in oil production has created additional jobs in related industries, such as pipeline construction. According to the Pipeline and Hazardous Materials Safety Administration, pipeline companies added 26,000 miles (41,843 km) of oil pipelines from 2012 to 2016. Several more pipeline projects are in the works, promising even more jobs. "It was an employer's market," says Willie Taylor, the executive director of the Permian Basin Workforce Development Board, a group that helps find employees for the energy sector. "Now it's more of a job seeker's market."[18]

> "[Fracking] has had incredibly positive impacts for the U.S. economy, for the workforce and even our reduced carbon footprint."[19]
>
> —John England, an energy analyst with Deloitte

In addition to creating jobs directly, fracking drives economic activity by lowering prices and putting more money into the hands of consumers. For example, gasoline prices have dropped 37 percent since 2008. That means that consumers have more money in their pockets to spend on other things. When the consumers spend that money, they help other businesses prosper, further fueling a broad economic expansion. "[Fracking] has had incredibly positive impacts for the U.S. economy, for the workforce and even our reduced carbon footprint,"[19] says John England, an energy analyst at financial consulting firm Deloitte. England's comment about a reduced carbon footprint refers to the fact that natural gas releases 58 percent less CO_2 than coal when burned.

Cleaner Energy

Fracking's role in reducing carbon emissions is significant. Fracking has released massive amounts of natural gas. And natural gas is much cleaner than coal. Every 1 million British thermal units of energy produced by natural gas emits 111 fewer pounds (50 kg) of CO_2 than the same amount of energy produced by coal. These savings add up. According to *Scientific American*, if the electricity from a 1-gigawatt coal-fired power plant is replaced by burning 35 billion cubic feet (1 billion cu. m) of natural gas instead, the annual savings of CO_2 is about 3.3 million tons (3 million metric tons).

This is not just theoretical. The EIA reports that nearly two-thirds of the reductions in energy-related CO_2 emissions since 2005 can be attributed to the use of natural gas rather than coal for electricity generation. "The underlying energy consumption trends that resulted in these changes—mainly because more electricity has been generated from natural gas than from other fossil fuels—have helped to lower the U.S. emissions level since 2005,"[20] states the EIA.

Lower greenhouse gas emissions are good not only for the environment but also for the economy, because they will help forestall or even prevent the costly effects of climate change. From energy independence to reduced emissions, fracking is making life better for all Americans.

Fracking Is Not a Good Way to Produce Fossil Fuels

"Fracking is bad because it releases methane; bad because it destabilizes fault lines; bad for pumping poisonous dreck into the ground; and of course, bad for climate change."

—Kevin Drum, political blogger and writer for *Mother Jones* magazine

Kevin Drum, "Fracking Is a Huge American Money Pit," *Mother Jones*, December 6, 2017. www.motherjones.com.

Consider these questions as you read:

1. Do you think fracking poses a danger to drinking water? Explain your answer.
2. Would you choose to live near a fracking site? Why or why not?
3. Are fracking-related earthquakes a major concern to you? Why or why not?

Editor's note: The discussion that follows presents common arguments made in support of this perspective, reinforced by facts, quotes, and examples taken from various sources.

Just when it seemed that the fossil fuel companies could not do any more to pollute the planet, they invented fracking, the riskiest and most dangerous drilling technique ever devised. Fracking pollutes the air and water, causes noise pollution, endangers human health, and triggers earthquakes. It must be stopped.

Endangering Water Supplies

Conventional fossil fuel drilling creates a vertical borehole through rock until a deposit of oil or natural gas is reached. The well is sealed, and the fossil fuels are pumped into tanks with very little spillage. Fracking, by contrast, bores a horizontal hole into a shale deposit and then fractures the rock by pumping in a slurry of water, chemicals, and sand or other materials. The fracturing of the rock is uncontrolled. Fissures can extend upward as much as 1,929 feet (588 m), according to researchers at Durham University in England. Such fractures can allow a witch's brew of contaminated water and fossil fuels to flow into the groundwater above. "Belowground pathways, including the production well itself and newly-created fractures, can allow hydraulic fracturing fluids or other fluids to reach underground drinking water resources,"[21] states a 2016 report from the US Environmental Protection Agency (EPA), an agency of the federal government.

Risks of Produced Water

Fracking fluids can also contaminate groundwater on the way out of a well. After the rock has been fractured, the pressure applied to the oil or gas well is released, and the direction of fluid flow reverses. The fluid that first returns to the surface is mostly the toxic mixture that was injected into the rock, sometimes called "flowback." The second type of fluid that returns to the surface contains oil and/or gas, which is then separated and processed. Both types of water are referred to as "produced water." If produced water is not contained within the drilling pipes, it can contaminate the groundwater on its way out of the well. It also can be spilled at the surface, contaminating surface water and sinking down to groundwater. According to an EPA study, 30 of the 225 documented produced water spills reached surface water, including creeks, ponds, and wetlands, and one was reported to have reached groundwater.

Even if produced water makes it safely out of the ground, it can contaminate the environment if a pipeline carrying it to a processing facility breaks. This is what happened in North Dakota in 2015. A broken pipe spilled 2.9 million gallons (11 million L) of produced water, which flowed into Blacktail Creek. The spill increased the concentration of chloride in the creek. High levels of chloride were also found downstream in the Little Muddy River and the Missouri River. Chloride and

Water Quality and Health Suffer Near Fracking Sites

Complaints of mysterious health problems have become commonplace among people who live near fracking sites. Studies have linked these problems to dangerously high levels of chemicals in the air and water. Bryan Latkanich allowed an energy company to begin fracking on his property in 2012. Soon after that he developed stomach problems and his son developed sores on his body. Tests conducted by Duquesne University in 2017 found that his well water had deteriorated since gas extraction began, with calcium forty-nine times higher, iron four times higher, sodium twice as high, and strontium seventeen times higher. This is just one of many documented examples of tainted water and health problems near fracking sites.

Baseline Data (2011)	Chemicals Found in Well Water	Test Results (2017)
1.90	Calcium	93.43
0.03	Iron	0.13
238.38	Sodium	510.38
0.18	Strontium	3.01

Measurements are in milligrams per liter

Source: Neela Banerjee and Inside Climate News, "Industrial Strength: How the U.S. Government Hid Fracking's Risks to Drinking Water," West Virginia Public Broadcasting, November 20, 2017. www.wvpublic.org.

other substances in produced water do not easily break down, or biodegrade. "Unlike spilled oil, which starts to break down in soil, these spilled brines consist of inorganic chemicals, metals and salts that are resistant to biodegradation,"[22] says Nancy Lauer, the lead author of a Duke University study that looked into the effects of the spill. According to another Duke University study, there were sixty-six hundred fracking spills in just four states from 2005 to 2014. This is pollution on a huge scale.

Health Concerns

Fluids are not the only harmful substances that escape from fracking sites. During fracking, toxic gases such as benzene are released from the rock. These gases mix with the atmosphere, polluting areas near the wells and causing health problems for energy workers and nearby residents. The operation of heavy equipment at a well site and the use of diesel trucks to transport materials to and from a site add to nearby air pollution. A 2016 study conducted by the Johns Hopkins Bloomberg School of Public Health found a link between fracking and increases in mild, moderate, and severe cases of asthma. The researchers found that asthma patients who live near fracking sites were 1.5 to 4.4 times more likely to have an asthma attack than those who live farther away. "Ours is the first to look at asthma, but we now have several studies suggesting adverse health outcomes related to the drilling of unconventional natural gas wells,"[23] says Sara G. Rasmussen, the scientist who led the study.

Fracking also affects infants born within 2 miles (3 km) of a well, according to a 2017 study published in *Science Advances*. The researchers reviewed the records of more than 1.1 million births in Pennsylvania from 2004 to 2013. They found that babies born to mothers who lived within 2 miles (3 km) of a fracking site during their pregnancies had more health problems than infants born farther away. The largest health impacts were discovered in infants whose mothers lived less than a mile (or kilometer) away from a fracking site. Living that close to a fracking site during pregnancy increased the odds of having a child with a low birth weight by 25 percent. Low birth weight is associated with many health and developmental problems later in life. "Informal estimates suggest that about 29,000 of the nearly 4 million annual U.S. births occur within 1 km of an active fracking site and that these births therefore may be at higher risk of poor birth outcomes,"[24] write the researchers.

> "About 29,000 of the nearly 4 million annual U.S. births occur within 1 km of an active fracking site and that these births therefore may be at higher risk of poor birth outcome."[24]
>
> —2017 study published in *Science Advances*

A separate study by Johns Hopkins University researchers looked at the birth records in Pennsylvania of 9,384 mothers who delivered 10,496 babies. The researchers found that women who lived near fracking sites had a 40 percent higher chance of having a premature baby and a 30 percent greater chance of having the pregnancy be classified as high risk. The researchers pointed to the impact of fracking on air quality, ground and surface water quality, and stress from noise as possible causes of the increased health risks for newborns. "This study adds to limited evidence that unconventional natural gas development adversely affects birth outcomes,"[25] write the researchers.

It is not just pregnant women who can be affected by the high amounts of noise caused by fracking. A 2017 study published in the *Science of the Total Environment*, a scientific journal, found that "oil and gas activities produce noise at levels that may increase the risk of adverse health outcomes, including annoyance, sleep disturbance, and cardiovascular disease."[26]

Earthquake Risks

The health hazards and environmental damage caused by fracking are extremely worrisome, but these are not the only problems associated with fracking. By disturbing rock formations far underground, fracking operations have been shown to induce earthquakes. According to a 2015 study by the US Geological Survey, a government agency, earthquakes with a magnitude equal to or greater than 3 have been increasing in the central United States (where most fracking occurs). The number has risen from an average of 24 per year in the years 1973–2008 to an average of 193 per year in 2009–2014, with 688 occurring in 2014 alone. Researchers have linked these earthquakes to fracking.

Some fracking-related earthquakes are even larger. The researchers report that fracking operations caused two magnitude 4.4 earthquakes in the Canadian provinces of Alberta and British Columbia in 2015 and a magnitude 5.6 earthquake in 2011 in Prague, Oklahoma. An earthquake that size could cause a great deal of damage if it occurs in a highly populated area. A study by the Federal Emergency Management Agency found that a magnitude 5.6 earthquake striking Dallas, Texas, which is located near the Barnett Shale formation where a great deal of fracking occurs, could damage eighty thousand buildings, cause levees to break, and lead to $9.5 billion in economic losses. Scientists also worry that moderate earthquakes caused by oil operations could trigger much larger ones located on major faults that are nearby.

Fracking is helping feed the American addiction to fossil fuels. It is polluting the environment and making people sick. And it has the potential to cause significant damage by inducing earthquakes. Fracking cannot be considered a good option for obtaining fossil fuels.

Chapter Three

Do Fossil Fuels Threaten the Environment?

Fossil Fuels Threaten the Environment

- The burning of fossil fuels is driving climate change.
- Fossil fuels are the major source of hazardous air pollution.
- Oil spills pollute the water and soil.
- The extraction of fossil fuels destroys habitat.

The Debate at a Glance

Fossil Fuels Do Not Threaten the Environment

- The impact of fossil fuels on climate change has been overstated.
- Oil spills do not pose long-term dangers to the environment.
- Fossil fuel–caused air pollution is declining in the United States.

Fossil Fuels Threaten the Environment

"Over the last century the burning of fossil fuels like coal and oil has increased the concentration of atmospheric carbon dioxide (CO_2)."

—NASA

NASA, "A Blanket Around the Earth," August 27, 2018. https://climate.nasa.gov.

Consider these questions as you read:

1. Do you think it is important to limit the output of CO_2? Why or why not?
2. Should oil and gas companies be allowed to expand their operations into remote and pristine environments? Why or why not?
3. How much responsibility for environmental damage should oil, gas, and mining companies have? Explain your answer.

Editor's note: The discussion that follows presents common arguments made in support of this perspective, reinforced by facts, quotes, and examples taken from various sources.

The earth's climate is changing. The atmosphere is warming, and that is triggering many other changes, including the warming of the land and oceans, the melting of glaciers and polar ice, and changes in ocean currents and weather patterns. These changes are known collectively as climate change. The earth's temperature has risen and fallen many times in its history, but this time is different. It is the first time that human activity is contributing to and even driving a change in global temperature. What are people doing that could have such an impact? They are burning fossil fuels.

When fossil fuels burn, they release various gases into the atmosphere, including CO_2 and nitrogen oxides. These gases help retain the sun's radiant energy as it enters the atmosphere from above and again as it is reflected from the earth below. The trapping of the sun's energy warms the planet. In fact, life as we know it could not exist without this warming effect. The sun's heat would escape into space, and earth would be too cold to sustain life. However, an overabundance of these gases is trapping more heat and causing the earth's temperature to rise. The phenomenon is known as global warming, and it is driving climate change.

Increasing CO_2

CO_2 levels today are higher than they have been at any time in the past eight hundred thousand years. Scientists know this because they have studied ice cores from the Antarctic ice pack. Air bubbles that formed in the glacial ice trapped tiny samples of atmospheric gases, providing a history of CO_2 levels. The amount of CO_2 in the atmosphere ranged between 175 parts per million and 300 parts per million for about eight hundred thousand years. However, since the late 1700s, when coal replaced wood as the world's primary source of global energy, atmospheric CO_2 has risen by 40 percent, surpassing 400 parts per million for the first time in human history.

> "Humans have increased atmospheric CO_2 concentration by more than a third since the Industrial Revolution began. This is the most important long-lived 'forcing' of climate change."[27]
>
> —NASA

It is not a coincidence that the amount of CO_2 in the atmosphere has skyrocketed since the burning of fossil fuels became the world's main source of energy. Various studies have shown that the rise in CO_2 is mainly attributable to the burning of fossil fuels. "Humans have increased atmospheric CO_2 concentration by more than a third since the Industrial Revolution began," states NASA. "This is the most important long-lived 'forcing' of climate change."[27]

According to the Union of Concerned Scientists, half of all human-related CO_2 emissions occurred in the past forty years. The EIA estimates that global energy-related CO_2 emissions rose by 6,658 million

Atmospheric CO$_2$ Rising Due to Fossil Fuels

Studies of Antarctic ice cores reveal that atmospheric CO$_2$ has increased to its highest level in the last 800,000 years, mainly due to the use of fossil fuels. Atmospheric CO$_2$ ranged from about 175 parts per million to 300 parts per million until fossil fuels came into use around 1750. Since then, atmospheric CO$_2$ has shot up to more than 400 parts per million, as indicated by the vertical line on the far right side of the graph. Most scientists believe the sudden increase in CO$_2$ is responsible for the rise in global temperatures, which is causing polar ice to melt, sea levels to rise, and other environmental changes.

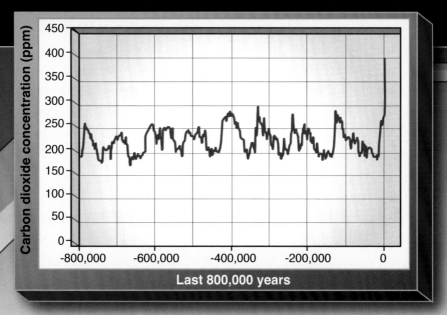

Source: Union of Concerned Scientists, "Why Does CO$_2$ Get Most of the Attention When There Are So Many Other Heat-Trapping Gases?," August 3, 2017. www.ucsusa.org.

tons (6,040 million metric tons), or 21 percent, from 2005 to 2017. Even worse, CO$_2$ persists in the atmosphere longer than other gases do. For example, water vapor dissipates within ten days; methane in about ten years; and nitrous oxide in one hundred years. By contrast, 40 percent of CO$_2$ emitted today will still be in the atmosphere in one hundred years; 20 percent will be in the atmosphere in one thousand years; and 10 percent will still be around in ten thousand years. "This literally means that the heat-trapping emissions we release today from our cars and power plants are setting the climate our children and grandchildren will inherit,"[28] states the Union of Concerned Scientists.

Polluting the Air

Climate change is just one of the negative effects of burning fossil fuels. Fossil fuel emissions include dangerous levels of carbon monoxide and ozone, which are a major source of air pollution. "Breathing ozone can trigger a variety of health problems including chest pain, coughing, throat irritation, and airway inflammation," states the EPA. "Ozone can worsen bronchitis, emphysema, and asthma, leading to increased medical care."[29]

Other air pollutants are released in the production of oil, gas, and coal. These include benzene, methane, and formaldehyde, all of which are highly toxic to humans. The air pollution emitted by coal and natural gas plants is linked with breathing problems, neurological damage, heart attacks, cancer, and premature death. According to the World Health Organization, about 4 million people die each year from outdoor air pollution.

Explosions, Leaks, and Spills

Fossil fuels also pose a danger to land and ocean environments. Oil pipelines that rupture, tankers that run aground, and undersea oil wells that leak all pose a danger to the environment. For example, in 2010 a natural gas leak on a floating drilling rig in the Gulf of Mexico caused an explosion. Eleven workers died in the explosion, and the drilling rig, known as *Deepwater Horizon*, sank. The underwater well spewed more than 4 million barrels of oil into the Gulf of Mexico. It was the largest oil spill in US waters. Oil sludge fouled more than 1,300 miles (2,092 km) of coastline, killing thousands of seabirds and other wildlife. Some oil remained suspended in the water, endangering sea creatures. As much as 20 percent of the oil sank to the ocean floor, damaging deep sea corals and microbes. A 2018 study found that eight years after the disaster, microbes were still being affected. "At the sites closest to the spill, biodiversity was flattened," says Leila Hamdan, a microbial ecologist at the University of Southern

Mississippi and lead author of the study. "It's premature to imagine that all the effects of the spill are over and remediated."[30]

Deepwater Horizon was not the first such oil spill, nor was it the last. A presidential commission that studied the *Deepwater Horizon* disaster found that there have been many similar accidents that could have been just as bad had it not been for good luck. "It's just not accurate to point to *Deepwater Horizon* and say, 'Well, this is just a strange and unprec-edented event unlikely to recur,'"[31] says Michael Bromwich, who served as the first director of the Bureau of Safety and Environmental Enforcement, an agency within the US Department of the Interior that oversees the offshore oil industry. Unfortunately, Bromwich has been proved right. In October 2017, for instance, a broken pipeline from an oil platform off the Louisiana coast leaked about sixteen thousand barrels of oil into the Gulf of Mexico in less than two days. Two days later, another explosion occurred off the coast of Louisiana, on a natural gas platform in Lake Pontchartrain, killing one worker and injuring seven more. Every time an accident occurs, oil companies say they are taking steps to prevent future disasters. And yet these disasters keep occurring. This is likely to become an even bigger problem as oil supplies run out and companies move farther offshore and into remote Arctic regions to find new sources of oil.

"The heat-trapping emissions we release today from our cars and power plants are setting the climate our children and grandchildren will inherit."[28]

—Union of Concerned Scientists

Destruction Caused by Extraction

Ecosystems and habitat suffer from the pursuit of fossil fuels as well. Energy companies clear the land where an oil well is to be located, known as the pad. They clear additional land to create access roads for vehicles coming in and out of the oil-production area. In some cases they build pipelines across pristine wilderness to move the crude oil to refineries and transport depots. The clearing of land for pipelines, roads, and oil wells destroys local ecosystems and can cause erosion of dirt and minerals into nearby waterways.

The destruction caused by open pit mines for coal, oil shale, and tar sands is even greater, destroying thousands of square miles of habitats worldwide. The process of extracting oil from shale and tar sands leaves behind enormous amounts of waste material, known as tailings, that contain heavy metals and toxic chemicals. These by-products cannot be buried, due to the dangers they pose to groundwater. They remain as scars on the land.

Fossil fuels are a source of pollution during the extraction process, during transport, and when they are burned for energy. Their climate-changing by-product, CO_2, lingers in the atmosphere for hundreds and even thousands of years. The pursuit and use of fossil fuels is hurting people, destroying habitats, polluting the air and water, and causing climate change.

Fossil Fuels Do Not Threaten the Environment

"CO_2—if you believe that the greenhouse gases do what some people say they do—is a greenhouse gas. Therefore, theoretically, increasing it in the atmosphere would cause some warming. The problem is there is no actual evidence of that."

—Patrick Moore, ecologist and cofounder of Greenpeace

Quoted in Jackie Daily, "Greenpeace Founder Takes Aim at Climate Change and CO_2 Fallacy," Blaze, November 3, 2017. www.theblaze.com.

Consider these questions as you read:

1. Do you believe that climate change is occurring and that fossil fuels are to blame? Explain your answer.
2. Should people be concerned about oil spill–related environmental damage in the face of research that has shown the resilience of nature after an oil spill? Explain your answer.
3. Under what conditions might the benefits of fossil fuels outweigh the detriments?

Editor's note: The discussion that follows presents common arguments made in support of this perspective, reinforced by facts, quotes, and examples taken from various sources.

Fossil fuels have been labeled public enemy number one in the climate change debate. Despite decades of research, there is little hard evidence to support this view. Although fossil fuels might contribute in some fashion to global warming, the impact of fossil fuels on climate change has been vastly overstated.

The premise of the global warming theory is that higher levels of CO_2 in the atmosphere are warming the planet. However, cores of sediments taken from the seafloor show that high levels of CO_2 do not precede warming trends; they follow them. "At the end of the last Ice Age, 10,000 years ago, carbon dioxide in the atmosphere rose dramatically as temperatures warmed,"[32] states NASA. This makes sense. More heat in the atmosphere causes the release of more CO_2 from the oceans and decomposing vegetation. NASA explains that prehistoric warming trends were touched off by changes in earth's orbit, not by increases in CO_2 levels. Ecologist Patrick Moore, one of the founders of the environmental organization Greenpeace, says:

There is some correlation, but little evidence, to support a direct causal relationship between CO_2 and global temperature through the millennia. The fact that we had both higher temperatures and an ice age at a time when CO_2 emissions were 10 times higher than they are today fundamentally contradicts the certainty that human-caused CO_2 emissions are the main cause of global warming.[33]

CO_2 Has Many Sources

Even if rising CO_2 levels do affect climate, fossil fuels are not the sole contributor to CO_2 increases. Global deforestation has consumed nearly 1 million square miles (2.6 million sq. km) of forests since 2000, preventing those plants from taking CO_2 out of the air. "By most accounts, deforestation in tropical rainforests adds more carbon dioxide to the atmosphere than the sum total of cars and trucks on the world's roads," state Roddy Scheer and Doug Moss, writers for *Scientific American*. "According to the World Carfree Network (WCN), cars and trucks account for about 14 percent of global carbon emissions, while most analysts attribute upwards of 15 percent to deforestation."[34] The IPCC states that the contribution of deforestation is even higher than that figure. According to the organization, one-third of human-caused CO_2 emissions since 1750 are the result of deforestation.

CO_2 is a colorless, odorless gas that human beings and animals exhale when they breathe. It is harmless to people, and it is necessary to plants. It is the gas plants "breathe" in and transform into the oxygen that humans and animals need. CO_2 has always been present in the world's atmosphere, and it is necessary for life.

CO_2 makes up a fraction of the atmosphere—and most of that (more than 96 percent) comes from natural sources. The world's oceans provide the greatest amount of CO_2, releasing dissolved CO_2 at the surface. Other sources of natural CO_2 include animal and human respiration and the decomposition of organic matter. Only about 3 percent of atmospheric CO_2 comes from human activity, and one-third of that is from deforestation. That means fossil fuel emissions produce just 2.6 percent of all the CO_2 in the atmosphere. That simply is not enough CO_2 to influence the climate one way or another.

> "By most accounts, deforestation in tropical rainforests adds more carbon dioxide to the atmosphere than the sum total of cars and trucks on the world's roads."[34]
>
> —Roddy Scheer and Doug Moss, writers for *Scientific American*

Fluctuations in natural CO_2 can be enormous. A 2017 study using data from NASA's Orbiting Carbon Observatory-2 found that rising temperatures caused by the climate cycle known as El Niño increased the amount of CO_2 released by the world's tropical forests by 2.5 billion tons (2.27 billion metric tons) per year. The warmer temperatures boosted the amount of CO_2 released by forest fires and decaying plants. This confirms the trends observed over millions of years: Warming increases CO_2, not the other way around. The world's climate is far too complex to say, as the IPCC does, that the burning of fossil fuels is the dominant cause of global warming. The sun, ocean currents, volcanic activity, forest fires, and deforestation all play a part.

Reduced Emissions

Fossil fuels are blamed not only for climate change but also for harmful air pollution. These claims are also exaggerated. When people hear that 4 million people die each year from outdoor air pollution, they usually think of cities polluted by auto emissions and coal burning. Contrary to popular belief, the most dangerous air pollutant does not come from fossil fuels. According to the World Health Organization, particulate matter (PM) poses by far the greatest danger to human health. PM comes from dust storms, forest fires, and human activities such as mining, garbage burning, and agriculture, not from the burning of fossil fuels. In fact, 3.8 million people a year die from breathing indoor PM created by heating and cooking with wood. Those lives could be saved if people heated and cooked with fossil fuel power instead of with wood.

In addition, new technologies are reducing outdoor air pollution. Automobile engines, clean coal plants, and combined cycle natural gas plants, which recycle heated wastewater to produce more energy with less gas, all are producing fewer emissions. As a result, greenhouse gas emissions are declining in the United States. According to the EPA, emissions of greenhouse gases (CO_2, methane, fluorinated gases, and nitrous oxide, which forms ozone) have declined for the past ten years and now stand at the lowest level since 1992. Most of this decrease is the result of reduced fossil fuel emissions. CO_2 emissions from fossil fuel combustion decreased by 861 million tons (781 million metric tons) from 2005 to 2016, a reduction of approximately 13.6 percent. If these emission-reducing technologies were adopted by all countries, the world could enjoy the benefits of fossil fuels and still have cleaner air.

The Resilience of the Sea

Fossil fuels are also blamed for fouling the oceans. Spills do occur. And although no one wants oil to spill into the oceans, the effects are often short lived. But the rapid recovery of sea life rarely gets as much attention as the initial effects of such spills. Just five years after the *Deepwater Horizon* oil spill, for instance, the numbers of fish caught had returned to pre-spill levels. Tests by the US Food and Drug Administration show no excess

Fossil Fuel Emissions Falling Fast

Thanks to technological advances, fossil fuel emissions have fallen since 1990. The amounts of dangerous chemicals in the air are now below EPA guidelines for clean air, known as the National Ambient Air Quality Standards (NAAQS), represented by the dotted gray line. This illustrates that people can use fossil fuels and enjoy clean air at the same time.

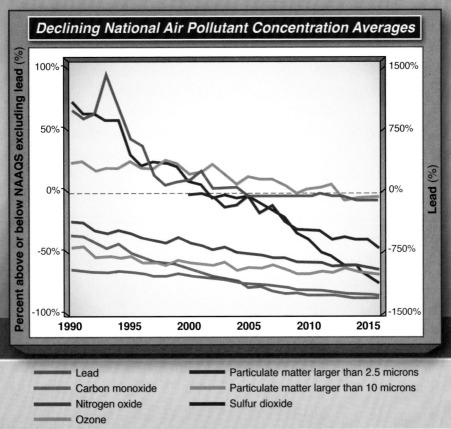

Declining National Air Pollutant Concentration Averages

Legend:
- Lead
- Carbon monoxide
- Nitrogen oxide
- Ozone
- Particulate matter larger than 2.5 microns
- Particulate matter larger than 10 microns
- Sulfur dioxide

Source: US Environmental Protection Agency, *Our Nation's Air: Status and Trends Through 2017,* 2017. https://gispub.epa.gov.

hydrocarbons in the region's seafood after the spill. Part of the reason for this was revealed in 2017, when researchers discovered that a naturally occurring underwater bacteria had consumed large amounts of the spilled oil. Thanks to the oil-eating microbe, larger species, including fish, shrimp, and crabs, have bounced back. "The actual marine life has recovered well from that spill, and fishing has resumed, so it has improved,"[35] says Gary Andersen, a microbial ecologist at the University of California and coauthor of the study that discovered the oil-eating microbes.

The reason that oil spills do not do long-term damage to the environment is that marine life is extremely adaptable. Many fish, shellfish, and other marine creatures produce huge numbers of eggs and larvae, which are widely distributed by currents. Normally, more than 99 percent of these eggs and larvae do not survive, due to competition from other organisms. However, when an oil spill wipes out large numbers of marine creatures, this overproduction strategy allows new organisms to fill the void left by the ones that have been killed. As a result, marine life bounces back quickly from even the worst oil spills.

The effects of fossil fuels on climate and the environment have been exaggerated. Environmental habitats are impacted by many forces but especially by deforestation and development. Fossil fuels are less complicated, however, and thus easier to blame. What is more, when fossil fuels do leak into the environment (as has happened in oil spills), research has shown nature's remarkable resilience. It is important to remember that oil, gas, and coal are not synthetic substances. They all occur naturally in the environment. According to Bernie Bernard of TDI-Brooks International, an offshore surface geochemical exploration company, there are likely more than fifty thousand seafloor seeps in the world's oceans. These natural upwellings release 4.3 million barrels of oil into the ocean waters each year, according to the National Research Council, and they have been doing so for millions of years with no long-term harmful effects on sea life. Equally important is the fact that the transportation, heating, and industries they fuel help feed the world and save lives. The value of fossil fuels far outweighs any harm they pose to the environment.

Chapter Four

Are Fossil Fuels Economical?

Fossil Fuels Are Economical

- New discoveries of fossil fuel deposits are increasing supply and decreasing prices.
- New technologies are making it cheaper and easier to extract fossil fuels.
- Infrastructure for handling fossil fuels already exists, keeping operating costs low, especially in comparison to renewables.

The Debate at a Glance

Fossil Fuels Are Not Economical

- Fossil fuel deposits are getting harder to find and develop, driving up costs.
- The cost of cleaning up oil spills further adds to the cost of fossil fuels.
- The impact of pollution on health care costs adds to the real cost of fossil fuels.

Fossil Fuels Are Economical

"U.S. energy policy should encourage investment in oil and gas, not because they already meet most of our energy needs but because they're affordable and reliable and essential for stability in the century ahead."

—Mark Perry, a scholar at the American Enterprise Institute and a professor of economics at the University of Michigan

Mark Perry, "Keeping Fossil Fuels Underground Makes No Sense," *U.S. News & World Report*, January 10, 2018. www.usnews.com.

Consider these questions as you read:

1. What is the relationship between fossil fuel supplies and cost?
2. How much weight should be given to cost when deciding energy policy? Explain your answer.
3. Should infrastructure needs be taken into account when comparing the costs of fossil fuels and renewable energy sources? Why or why not?

Editor's note: The discussion that follows presents common arguments made in support of this perspective, reinforced by facts, quotes, and examples taken from various sources.

In July 2018 the EIA reported that the per capita (per person) spending for energy in the United States hit its lowest level since 1970, decreasing 9 percent from 2015 to 2016. This was not due to a reduction in energy consumption, which remained unchanged. And it was not due to a sudden surge in the use of wind or solar power. Instead, it was caused by a historic drop in the cost of fossil fuels. This savings in energy costs put real money into the pockets of consumers, who were free to spend it on other things, improving their quality of life and fueling the country's economic growth.

Gasoline Prices Unchanged for Forty-Three Years

Despite persistent warnings about oil scarcity and rising prices, the average price of a gallon of gasoline is the same now as it was forty-three years ago in inflation-adjusted dollars. The average price in 1976 was $2.72 per gallon, and the average price in 2018 was $2.77 per gallon. The US Energy Information Administration has estimated an average price in 2019 of $2.71 per gallon. And, with cars getting more miles to the gallon than ever before, the cost per mile has dropped. Fossil fuels are clearly economical.

Regular Gasoline Retail Prices

Source: US Energy Information Administration, "Real Prices Viewer," August 7, 2018. www.eia.gov.

Fossil Fuel Supply and Demand

Market prices of fuel—just like prices for anything else—are governed by the law of supply and demand. If the supply of something is low but the demand is high, the price increases. However, if the supply is high and the demand is low, the price decreases. Currently, there is both a large supply of fossil fuels and a low demand. These forces have combined to drive fossil fuel prices to their lowest levels in many years.

The current levels of fossil fuel supply and demand are something of a surprise. For decades, energy experts have been predicting that the supply of fossil fuels would decrease and the demand would increase, driving prices to unsustainable levels. "The oil and natural gas that we rely on for 75 percent of our energy are simply running out," President Jimmy Carter told the nation in a televised address on April 18, 1977. He urged Americans to conserve energy, stating that if consumption continued to rise by even 5 percent a year, "we could use up all the proven reserves of oil in the entire world by the end of the next decade." Without conservation, the prices would skyrocket. "Within 10 years, we would not be able to import enough oil from any country, at any acceptable price,"[36] Carter said.

Despite Carter's warning, global energy consumption has continued to grow, and the world has not run out of fossil fuels. On the contrary, energy consumption was 91 percent higher in 2017 than it was in 1977, yet fossil fuel reserves are nowhere near being depleted. This is due in part to major oil discoveries made in Brazil, Canada, Kazakhstan, Mexico, Russia, and the North Sea. In fact, there is such an abundance of fossil fuels today that oil actually costs less now than when Carter made his dire predictions about runaway prices.

> "There is a quiet revolution brewing in the East Mediterranean. . . . Only mentioned in tiny hiccups in our newspapers one of the most gigantic discoveries ever made of natural oil and gas under the East Mediterranean will soon be coming on stream."[37]
>
> —Frederick Forsyth, author and commentator

Huge supplies of natural gas have also been found. Two years after Carter's speech, Qatar began producing natural gas from a field that holds 896 trillion cubic feet (25.4 trillion cu. m) of natural gas, or 14 percent of the world's supply. In April 2018 a natural gas field was discovered off the coasts of Turkey, Lebanon, Cyprus, Israel, and Egypt, estimated to contain 122 trillion cubic feet (3.5 trillion cu. m) of natural gas. Author and commentator Frederick Forsyth writes:

You do not have to be an eco-geologist or international financier —both of which I am emphatically not—to realise there is a quiet revolution brewing in the East Mediterranean. I refer not to the Syrian civil war nor Russia's naked imperialism in that zone but to something happening far beneath those blue touristic waves. Only mentioned in tiny hiccups in our newspapers one of the most gigantic discoveries ever made of natural oil and gas under the East Mediterranean will soon be coming on stream.[37]

These enormous deposits in Asia and the Middle East are keeping natural gas prices low.

The Shale Revolution

The recent reduction in fossil fuel prices is largely a result of shale oil production, a process made possible by advances in extraction technology. Fracking has led to a dramatic increase in fossil fuel supplies, which in turn has resulted in a significant decrease in costs. Thanks to its enormous shale oil deposits, the United States has surpassed Saudi Arabia and Russia to become the nation with the world's largest oil reserves, according to a 2016 study by Rystad Energy, an energy consulting company based in Oslo, Norway. Rystad pegs US oil reserves at 264 billion barrels, compared to Russia's 256 billion and Saudi Arabia's 212 billion.

The shale revolution is a global phenomenon. There are more than six hundred known shale oil deposits in thirty-three countries on all continents. In 2011 the Israel Energy Initiatives announced that shale formations in Israel's Shfela basin contain 40 billion barrels of oil. In April 2018 the island nation of Bahrain announced that it had discovered a shale reserve with at least 80 billion barrels of crude oil. The new oil field in Bahrain also contains an estimated 14 trillion cubic feet (396 billion cu. m) of gas. A 2016 report by the World Energy Council, a London-based global energy forum, reports that the world's oil shale resources contain around 6 trillion barrels of shale oil, which is four times more than all of the world's known conventional crude oil reserves combined.

The surge in shale oil production has caused the price of crude oil to drop by 75 percent from 2011 to 2016, from $113 dollars a barrel to just $29 per barrel. Cheaper oil has led to cheaper gasoline. Average gas prices peaked at $3.98 per gallon in 2012 and were projected to fall to just $2.77 in 2019. In fact, gasoline costs less now than it did one hundred years ago, according to InflationData, which calculates gas prices based on current dollar values. In 1918 gasoline sold for $3.92 per gallon in today's dollars. Even at the depths of the Great Depression, when prices for everything fell, gasoline cost about the same as it does today—$2.65 per gallon. Overall, the average price of a gallon of gas over the past one hundred years was $2.64 per gallon, about the same as today's prices. Clearly, claims of rising fossil fuel costs are a myth.

Existing Infrastructure Affects Cost

The price of oil is only meaningful in relation to the price of other energy sources. If something came along that could produce the same amount of energy as fossil fuels at a lower cost, then that source would eventually replace fossil fuels. Some renewables, such as land-based wind turbines, can produce electricity at a lower cost than any fossil fuel, because its "fuel," wind, is free. However, the cost of building enough wind turbines, solar panels, hydroelectric dams, and even nuclear reactors to replace fossil fuels would be astronomical. Those infrastructure costs must be recovered, and they are reflected in renewable energy prices. By contrast, most of the infrastructure needed to bring fossil fuels to consumers already exists. The wells, pipelines, tankers, railcars, refineries, holding tanks, and service stations have already been built. Because this infrastructure is in place, any increase in fossil fuel supply leads to lower prices almost immediately.

> "While anti-fossil initiatives raise the cost of using them, their dominance continues because they are abundant, relatively cheap, and have a high energy density."[38]
>
> —William O'Keefe, CEO of the George C. Marshall Institute

Another reason fossil fuel prices have fallen is that demand has leveled off in North America and Europe. Government mandates to create more fuel-efficient automobiles and energy-efficient appliances have allowed the industrialized nations to make better use of their fossil fuels. Efficiencies have come to air conditioners, refrigerators, and other appliances. At the same time, computer-controlled "smart" homes are reducing energy consumption by turning off lights and electronic devices when users are not in a room and by automatically controlling room temperatures. Advanced technology is helping slow increases in energy demand, which keeps the cost of fossil fuels low.

Fossil fuels contain the greatest amount of energy by volume (energy density) of all substances on earth, except for nuclear materials such as uranium, plutonium, and hydrogen. And they are incredibly abundant and affordable. "While anti-fossil initiatives raise the cost of using them, their dominance continues because they are abundant, relatively cheap, and have a high energy density," writes William O'Keefe, CEO of the George C. Marshall Institute, a nonprofit think tank. "No alternative can compete economically with those qualities, without large government subsidies."[38]

Fossil Fuels Are Not Economical

"Turning to renewables for new power generation is not simply an environmentally conscious decision, it is now—overwhelmingly—a smart economic one."

—Adnan Amin, director-general of the International Renewable Energy Agency

Quoted in Dominic Dudley, "Renewable Energy Will Be Consistently Cheaper than Fossil Fuels by 2020, Report Claims," *Forbes*, January 13, 2018. www.forbes.com.

Consider these questions as you read:

1. What are the factors driving up the costs of fossil fuels?
2. Is it fair to compare the costs of renewable energy sources and fossil fuels? Why or why not?
3. Do you think hidden costs such as health problems and disaster clean-up should be factored into the cost of using fossil fuels? Why or why not?

Editor's note: The discussion that follows presents common arguments made in support of this perspective, reinforced by facts, quotes, and examples taken from various sources.

Fossil fuels are expensive now and will only get more expensive in the future. Some of these costs are obvious, such as the price people pay for electricity. These are known as direct costs. Other costs are hidden, such as the costs to the environment or to human health. The combination of direct and indirect costs will make fossil fuels unaffordable in the future.

Direct Costs

The direct costs of fossil fuels are destined to rise over the long haul. As reserves of fossil fuels are used up, the oil- and gas-producing nations will raise their prices to squeeze the maximum profit out of the reserves they have left. Replacing the existing reserves with new ones will become

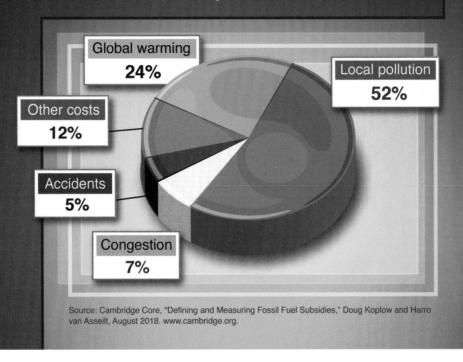

The Hidden Costs of Fossil Fuels

The International Monetary Fund (IMF) calculates the hidden costs of using fossil fuels. This chart gives a breakdown of those costs. The largest category is health care costs related to pollution from fossil fuels, followed by costs from the impacts of global warming, including rising sea levels and violent storms. Costs related to traffic congestion, accidents, and other sources make up the remainder. These hidden costs make fossil fuels a bad bargain.

Global warming
24%

Local pollution
52%

Other costs
12%

Accidents
5%

Congestion
7%

Source: Cambridge Core, "Defining and Measuring Fossil Fuel Subsidies," Doug Koplow and Harro van Asseilt, August 2018. www.cambridge.org.

increasingly costly as drilling moves farther offshore into deeper water and farther into remote land-based locations. Finding the new fossil fuel reserves, extracting them, and transporting them will add so much cost to fossil fuels that they will not be able to compete with renewables.

Right now, fossil fuel prices are low because companies have learned how to extract oil from shale deposits. However, the cost of recovering shale oil has only recently dropped to the point that the process is profitable. That is because fracking requires large amounts of expensive chemicals to separate the fossil fuels from the stone. The high cost of these chemicals, along with the labor, equipment, and energy needed to fracture the rock and force out the oil and gas, means that the cost of fracking cannot decrease any further. As a result, the price of shale oil cannot fall any more than it already has.

Meanwhile, the opposite is true of renewables. The direct costs of renewable energy have tumbled in recent years and now rival and in some cases beat the direct costs of fossil fuels. The EIA estimates that electricity from a new photovoltaic solar farm entering service in 2022 would be 4.65 cents per kWh, while energy from a new natural gas plant entering service at the same time would be 4.81 cents per kWh. Because the operation of solar farms is so cheap, some power companies are bidding on contracts to produce twenty to thirty years of electricity for even less than the EIA estimates. "Large solar plants in very sunny parts of the world, like the Atacama Desert in Chile, can build solar for under 3 cents per kWh today," says Jenny Chase of Bloomberg New Energy Finance. "The costs of solar energy have come down much faster and the volumes risen much more quickly than we ever dreamed was possible."[39]

> "The costs of solar energy have come down much faster and the volumes risen much more quickly than we ever dreamed was possible."[39]
>
> —Jenny Chase, head of solar analysis at Bloomberg New Energy Finance

The Hidden Costs of Fossil Fuels

The cost of renewables is concentrated in the materials and labor used to build the solar and wind farms. Once they are up and running, the costs are low. Their fuel—sunlight and wind—is free. Labor and maintenance costs are low. In addition, renewable sources do not create air, water, or soil pollution as a by-product of generating power. As a result, there are no costs related to cleanups or health hazards. The opposite is true of fossil fuel energy production. Its greatest cost is in the fuel consumed—coal, oil, and natural gas. Fossil fuel power plants also require a great deal of labor and maintenance. Most importantly, fossil fuel production and use create large amounts of air, water, and soil pollution. This pollution comes at a price that is not reflected in the direct costs of the energy. Instead, it is paid by individuals' health, by insurance companies, and by government. These are the indirect costs of fossil fuels.

One of the greatest hidden costs of fossil fuels is pollution. The depletion of existing oil and gas reserves will force energy companies to look for new reserves to take their place. This will require drilling under more difficult conditions that increase the likelihood of environmental disasters, including spills from underwater wells, breaks in pipelines leading up to the drilling platforms, and explosions on the platforms themselves, as occurred in the *Deepwater Horizon* disaster of 2010. In addition, oil tankers can sink or run aground, as the *Exxon Valdez* did in 1989, spilling about 250,000 barrels of oil into Prince William Sound, off the coast of Alaska.

These disasters are extremely costly. The *Exxon Valdez* spill cost Exxon $3.5 billion ($6.3 billion in today's dollars) in cleanup costs, fines, and lawsuit settlements. The *Deepwater Horizon* spill cost BP much more. The company reports that it spent $40 billion to stop the leak and clean up the spill. In addition, BP had to pay several billion dollars more in fines and lawsuit settlements. The British newspaper the *Guardian* reported in January 2018 that BP's final bill for *Deepwater Horizon* was $65 billion. The companies responsible for the disasters initially pay for the disasters, but the costs are later passed on to consumers in the form of higher prices.

The use of fossil fuels costs human lives as well. Eleven people died in the *Deepwater Horizon* explosion. According to the Bureau of Safety and Environmental Enforcement, the *Deepwater Horizon* workers were among thirty-four workers who lost their lives in offshore drilling rig accidents from 2008 to 2012. Oil workers are seven times more likely than the average US worker to die on the job, according the Centers for Disease Control and Prevention. Coal miners also face significant dangers. According to the US Department of Labor, 315 coal miners died in coal mine accidents from January 2005 to March 2018. This includes twenty-nine miners who were killed in an explosion at the Upper Big Branch Mine in West Virginia in 2010.

Health Care Costs

The on-the-job death toll of fossil fuel workers is tragic, but accidents are not the only or even the main cause of death related to the fossil fuel industries. According the US Department of Labor, more than seventy-six thousand coal miners have died of black lung since 1968. Black lung is a chronic, progressive, disabling, and often fatal lung disease. It is caused by inhaling coal mine dust, a mix of particles, including coal, silica, and iron. The coal dust settles in the lungs and causes them to harden, making breathing difficult. The disease was thought to have been eliminated through safety procedures, but in February 2018, the National Institute for Occupational Safety and Health identified the largest cluster of advanced black lung disease ever reported. A total of 416 cases were reported in three clinics in Kentucky, Virginia, and West Virginia from 2013 to 2017.

> "Fossil-fuel combustion by-products are the world's most significant threat to children's health."[40]
>
> —Frederica P. Perera, a public health researcher at Columbia University

Breathing air pollution from the burning of fossil fuels takes a toll on health as well. A study by the nonprofit Clean Air Task Force found that fine particle pollution from US coal plants resulted in 13,200 deaths, 9,700 hospitalizations, and 20,000 heart attacks each year, resulting in $100 billion in health care costs. A different study, this one by the EPA, found that the cost of illnesses, premature death, lost time at work, and health care due to fossil fuel pollution added thirty-two cents per kWh to the price of coal-generated electricity, thirteen cents per kWh to the price of oil, and two cents per kWh to the price of natural gas.

Pollution is especially dangerous for infants and children, whose bodies are still developing, according to Frederica P. Perera, a public health researcher at Columbia University. This is especially true of babies developing inside their mothers prior to birth, known as being in utero. "Fossil-fuel combustion by-products are the world's most significant threat to children's health," writes Perera. "Impacts include impairment of cognitive and behavioral development, respiratory illness, and other chronic diseases—all of which may be 'seeded' in utero and affect health and functioning immediately and over the life course."[40]

The nation's and the world's dependence on fossil fuels has many costs—some direct and others hidden. When these costs are taken as a whole, it becomes clear that fossil fuels are a costly form of energy that humanity cannot afford.

Source Notes

Overview: Fossil Fuels

1. R.K. Pachauri and L.A. Meyer, eds., *Climate Change 2014: Synthesis Report*. Geneva: Intergovernmental Panel on Climate Change, 2014, p. 4. www .ipcc.ch.
2. Quoted in Jane A. Legget, "Evolving Assessments of Human and Natural Contributions to Climate Change," Congressional Research Service, February 1, 2018, p. 13. https://fas.org.
3. Nicole Lewis, "EPA Administrator Scott Pruitt's Claim That the U.S. Is 'Leading the World' in 'CO_2 Footprint' Reductions," *Washington Post*, October 23, 2017. www.washingtonpost.com.

Chapter One: Should the World Stop Using Fossil Fuels?

4. Lee R. Raymond, "Ethics, Enterprise, and the Multinational Corporation," Acton Institute, July 20, 2010. https://acton.org.
5. *Economist*, "Can the World Thrive on 100% Renewable Energy?," July 13, 2017. www.economist.com.
6. Robert Bryce, "Bad News for Green Energy Lovers: US Oil & Gas Are Booming," *New York Post*, May 17, 2018. https://nypost.com.
7. Matt Ridley, "Fossil Fuels Will Save the World (Really)," *Wall Street Journal*, March 13, 2015. www.wsj.com.
8. Lazard, "Lazard Releases Annual Levelized Cost of Energy and Levelized Cost of Storage Analyses," November 2, 2017. www.lazard.com.
9. Donald J. Weubbles et al., *Climate Science Special Report: Fourth National Climate Assessment*, vol. 1. Washington, DC: US Global Change Research Program, 2017, p. 412. https://science2017.globalchange.gov.
10. Lazard, "Lazard Releases Annual Levelized Cost of Energy and Levelized Cost of Storage Analyses."
11. Quoted in Tom Randall, "World Energy Hits a Turning Point: Solar That's Cheaper than Wind," Bloomberg, December 15, 2016. www.bloomberg .com.
12. Jenny Chase, interview with the author, July 7, 2018.
13. Quoted in Gary Peters, "Hybrid Vessels: Here to Stay, or Fleeting Trend?," Ship Technology, March 27, 2017. www.ship-technology.com.

14. Quoted in Fred Lambert, "Elon Musk: More than Half of New Vehicles Will Be Electric and Almost All Autonomous in the US Within 10 Years," Electrek, July 15, 2017. https://electrek.co.

Chapter Two: Is Fracking a Good Way to Produce Fossil Fuels?

15. Quoted in Sheila Olson, "Chesapeake Sets Record with Massive Frack (CHK)," Investopedia, October 21, 2016. www.investopedia.com.

16. Mark P. Mills, "Testimony Before the U.S. Senate Energy and Natural Resources Committee," Manhattan Institute, July 18, 2017. www.manhattan-institute.org.

17. Quoted in Vauhini Vara, "How Frackers Beat OPEC," *Atlantic*, February 2017. www.theatlantic.com.

18. Quoted in Liz Hampton, "U.S. Oil Industry Set to Break Record, Upend Global Trade," Reuters, January 16, 2018. www.reuters.com.

19. Quoted in Hampton, "U.S. Oil Industry Set to Break Record, Upend Global Trade."

20. Perry Lindstrom, "U.S. Energy-Related CO_2 Emissions Expected to Rise Slightly in 2018, Remain Flat in 2019," US Energy Information Administration, February 8, 2018. www.eia.gov.

21. US Environmental Protection Agency, *Hydraulic Fracturing for Oil and Gas: Impacts from the Hydraulic Fracturing Water Cycle on Drinking Water Resources in the United States*. Washington, DC: Office of Research and Development, 2016, p. 25. www.epa.gov.

22. Quoted in Amy Dalrymple, "Spill Contamination Lingering Years Later, Study Says," *Billings (MT) Gazette*, April 30, 2016. https://billingsgazette.com.

23. Quoted in Meredith Cohn, "Fracking Linked to Asthma Attacks in Hopkins Study," *Baltimore Sun*, August 5, 2016. www.baltimoresun.com.

24. Janet Currie et al., "Hydraulic Fracturing and Infant Health: New Evidence from Pennsylvania," *Science Advances*, December 13, 2017. http://advances.sciencemag.org.

25. Joan A. Casey et al., "Unconventional Natural Gas Development and Birth Outcomes in Pennsylvania, USA," *Epidemiology*, March 2016. www.ncbi.nlm.nih.gov.

26. Jake Hays et al., "Public Health Implications of Environmental Noise Associated with Unconventional Oil and Gas Development," *Science of the Total Environment*, February 15, 2017. www.sciencedirect.com.

Chapter Three: Do Fossil Fuels Threaten the Environment?

27. NASA, "A Blanket Around the Earth," July 23, 2018. https://climate.nasa.gov.

28. Union of Concerned Scientists, "Why Does CO_2 Get Most of the Attention When There Are So Many Other Heat-Trapping Gases?," August 3, 2017. www.ucsusa.org.

29. US Environmental Protection Agency, "Basic Information About Ozone," 2018. www.epa.gov.

30. Quoted in Oliver Milman, "Deepwater Horizon Disaster Altered Building Blocks of Ocean Life," *Guardian* (Manchester), June 28, 2018. www.theguardian.com.

31. Quoted in Jie Jenny Zou, "8 Years After Deepwater Horizon Explosion, Is Another Disaster Waiting to Happen?," NPR, April 20, 2018. www.npr.org.

32. NASA Earth Observatory, "Changes in the Carbon Cycle," June 16, 2011. https://earthobservatory.nasa.gov.

33. Quoted in Ted Thornhill, "Humans Are NOT to Blame for Global Warming, Says Greenpeace Co-Founder, as He Insists There Is 'No Scientific Proof' Climate Change Is Manmade," *Daily Mail* (London), February 27, 2014. www.dailymail.co.uk.

34. Roddy Scheer and Doug Moss, "Deforestation and Its Extreme Effect on Global Warming," *Scientific American*, 2018. www.scientificamerican.com.

35. Quoted in Robert Ferris, "Much of the Deepwater Horizon Oil Spill Has Disappeared Because of Bacteria," CNBC, June 26, 2017. www.cnbc.com.

Chapter Four: Are Fossil Fuels Economical?

36. Jimmy Carter, "Full Text of 'Executive Energy Documents,'" Internet Archive, April 20, 1977. https://archive.org.

37. Frederick Forsyth, "Will Israel Be the Next Big Oil Power? Asks Frederick Forsyth," *Daily Express* (London), April 20, 2018. www.express.co.uk.

38. William O'Keefe, "Fossil Fuels Are Here to Stay," Economics 21, July 30, 2015. https://economics21.org.

39. Chase interview.

40. Frederica P. Perera, "Pollution from Fossil-Fuel Combustion Is the Leading Environmental Threat to Global Pediatric Health and Equity: Solutions Exist," *International Journal of Environmental Research and Public Health*, December 23, 2017. www.ncbi.nlm.nih.gov.

Fossil Fuel Facts

Fossil Fuel Production

- Global oil production reached 92.6 million barrels per day in 2017, the highest level in history.
- In 2017 global oil production increased for the eighth straight year.
- The United States is the world's leading crude oil producer, with production averaging 10.7 million barrels per day in 2018, according to the EIA.
- Global natural gas production increased 3 percent in 2017 to a new record of 355 billion cubic feet (10 billion cu. m) per day.
- Natural gas is the world's fastest-growing fossil fuel, increasing by 1.4 percent per year, compared with liquid's 0.7 percent per year growth and virtually no growth in coal use (0.1 percent per year), according to the EIA.

Fossil Fuel Consumption

- The share of fossil fuel energy consumption fell from 94.6 percent of the world's total energy use in 1969 to 80 percent in 2016, according to the EIA.
- In 2017 fossil fuel consumption in the US electric power sector declined to 22.5 quadrillion British thermal units, the lowest level since 1994, according to the EIA.
- Oil is the world's leading fuel, accounting for a third of global energy consumption, according to BP.
- Global consumption of coal fell by 1.7 percent in 2016, the second successive annual decline.
- Coal's share of global primary energy consumption fell to 28.1 percent in 2016, the lowest share since 2004, according to the EIA.
- China is the world's top coal consumer, using 50.7 percent of the world's coal in 2017, according to BP.

Fossil Fuel Emissions

- Global CO_2 emissions rose 1.6 percent in 2017 to a new record of 36.8 billion tons (33.4 billion metric tons), according to BP.
- CO_2 emissions declined by one-half of 1 percent (0.5 percent) in the United States in 2017 as more coal-fired power was phased out, according to BP.
- CO_2 emissions from the US electric power sector in 2017 were the lowest since 1987, according to the EIA.
- CO_2 emissions rose in the Asia-Pacific region, Europe, and Africa in 2017, according to BP.
- Of the eighteen Asia-Pacific countries reported, only Japan showed a decline in CO_2 emissions in 2017, according to BP.

Climate Change

- Global annually averaged surface air temperature has increased by about 1.8°F (1.0°C) over the past 115 years (1901–2016), according to the US Global Change Research Program.
- The likely range of the human contribution to the global mean temperature increase from 1951 to 2010 is 1.1°F to 1.4°F (0.6°C to 0.8°C).
- The current period is now the warmest in the history of modern civilization.
- Global average sea level has risen by about 7 to 8 inches (17.8 to 20.3 cm) since 1900, with almost half (about 3 inches, or 7.6 cm) of that rise occurring since 1993.

Related Organizations and Websites

American Petroleum Institute (API)
1220 L St. NW
Washington, DC 20005
website: www.api.org

The API represents America's petroleum industry. Its activities include lobbying, conducting research, and setting technical standards for the petroleum industry. It publishes numerous position papers, reports, and information sheets.

Energy Conservation Coalition (ECC)
1525 New Hampshire Ave. NW
Washington, DC 20036

This group of public interest organizations promotes energy conservation. The ECC publishes *Powerline*, a bimonthly periodical covering consumer issues on energy and utilities.

Energy Information Administration (EIA)
1000 Independence Ave. SW
Washington, DC 20585
website: www.eia.gov

The EIA is the federal agency responsible for collecting, analyzing, and disseminating energy information and promoting sound policies. Its home page and Today in Energy section feature nearly daily reports on energy consumption, use, and trends, featuring easy-to-read charts and graphs.

Friends of the Earth
1025 Vermont Ave. NW, Suite 300
Washington, DC 20005
website: www.foe.org

Friends of the Earth is an environmental group dedicated to the well-being and protection of the natural world. Its website offers news updates on environmental concerns and a library of free publications available as PDF files.

Intergovernmental Panel on Climate Change (IPCC)
c/o World Meteorological Organization
7bis Avenue de la Paix
C.P. 2300
CH-1211 Geneva 2, Switzerland
website: www.ipcc.ch

The IPCC is the international body for assessing the science related to climate change. It provides policy makers with regular assessments of the scientific basis of climate change, its impacts and future risks, and options for addressing it. The IPCC works with leading scientists worldwide to assess the published research of thousands of climate scientists.

The National Renewable Energy Laboratory (NREL)
1617 Cole Blvd.
Golden, CO 80401-3393
website: www.nrel.gov

The NREL specializes in renewable energy and energy efficiency research and development. It is operated by a private entity on behalf of the federal government, which also funds its work. Its website features free publications, news and feature stories about renewable energy, and an area for students and teachers.

Union of Concerned Scientists
2 Brattle Square
Cambridge, MA 02138
website: www.ucsusa.org

The Union of Concerned Scientists combines technical analysis and advocacy to create innovative, practical solutions for a healthy, safe, and sustainable future. Its website contains informative sections devoted to clean energy, clean vehicles, and global warming.

US Environmental Protection Agency (EPA)
Ariel Rios Building
1200 Pennsylvania Ave. NW
Washington, DC 20460
website: www.epa.gov

The EPA is the federal agency in charge of protecting the environment and controlling pollution. The agency works toward these goals by enacting and enforcing regulations, identifying and fining polluters, assisting businesses and local environmental agencies, and cleaning up polluted sites.

For Further Research

Books

Michelle Bamberger and Robert Oswald, *The Real Cost of Fracking*. Boston: Beacon, 2015.

Anne C. Cunningham, ed., *Critical Perspectives on Fossil Fuels vs. Renewable Energy*. New York: Enslow, 2017.

Russell Gold, *The Boom: How Fracking Ignited the American Energy Revolution and Changed the World*. New York: Simon & Schuster, 2015.

Eve Hartman and Wendy Meshbesher, *Fossil Fuels*. Chicago: Raintree, 2016.

Sherri Mabry-Gordon, *Out of Gas: Using Up Fossil Fuels*. New York: Enslow, 2016.

Gary Sernovitz, *The Green and the Black: The Complete Story of the Shale Revolution, the Fight Over Fracking, and the Future of Energy*. New York: St. Martin's, 2016.

Varun Sivaram, *Taming the Sun*. Boston: MIT Press, 2018.

Internet Sources

BP, *BP Statistical Review of World Energy, 2018*. London: BP, 2018. www.bp.com/content/dam/bp/en/corporate/pdf/energy-economics/statistical-review/bp-stats-review-2018-full-report.pdf.

International Energy Agency, *Global Energy & CO_2 Status Report, 2017*. Paris: International Energy Agency, 2018. www.iea.org/publications/freepublications/publication/GECO2017.pdf.

Lazard, "Levelized Cost of Energy 2017," November 2, 1017. www.lazard.com/perspective/levelized-cost-of-energy-2017.

US Energy Information Administration, *International Energy Outlook, 2017*. Washington, DC: US Energy Information Administration, 2017. www.eia.gov/outlooks/archive/ieo17/pdf/0484(2017).pdf.

US Energy Information Administration, *International Energy Outlook, 2018*. Washington, DC: US Energy Information Administration, 2018. www.eia.gov/outlooks/ieo.

Donald J. Weubbles et al., *Climate Science Special Report: Fourth National Climate Assessment*, vol. 1. Washington, DC: US Global Change Research Program, 2017. https://science2017.globalchange.gov/down loads/CSSR2017_FullReport.pdf.

About the Author

Bradley Steffens is a poet, a novelist, and an award-winning author of more than forty nonfiction books for children and young adults.